INTENTIONAL FITNESS
WORKING OUT YOUR SALVATION

MARY GRAZIANO SCRO

Seattle WA 2015

Copyright 2015 Mary Graziano Scro

This work is licensed under a Creative Commons Attribution-Noncommercial-No Derivative Works 3.0 Unported License. **Attribution** — You must attribute the work in the manner specified by the author or licensor (but not in any way that suggests that they endorse you or your use of the work). **Noncommercial** — You may not use this work for commercial purposes. **No Derivative Works** — You may not alter, transform, or build upon this work.

**Inquiries about additional permissions
should be directed to: info@booktrope.com**

Cover Design by Jennifer Givner

Previously self-published as *Intentional Fitness:
Working Out Your Salvation so Others Can See Jesus*, 2013

Print ISBN 978-1-62015-848-7
EPUB ISBN 978-1-62015-869-2
Library of Congress Control Number: 2015941169

Unless otherwise noted, all Scriptures are taken from the Holy Bible, New International Version®, NIV®. Copyright © 1973, 1978, 1984, 2011 by Biblica, Inc.™ Used by permission of Zondervan. All rights reserved worldwide. http://www.zondervan.com The "NIV" and "New International Version" are trademarks registered in the United States Patent and Trademark Office by Biblica, Inc.™

Scripture quotations marked NLT are taken from the *Holy Bible*, New Living Translation, copyright ©1996, 2004, 2007, 2013 by Tyndale House Foundation. Used by permission of Tyndale House Publishers, Inc., Carol Stream, Illinois 60188. All rights reserved. • Scripture references marked NKJV are taken from the New King James Version®. Copyright © 1982 by Thomas Nelson. Used by permission. All rights reserved. • Scripture quotations marked AMP are taken from the Amplified Bible, Copyright © 1954, 1958, 1962, 1964, 1965, 1987 by The Lockman Foundation. Used by permission. • Scripture quotations marked MSG are from THE MESSAGE. Copyright © by Eugene H. Peterson 1993, 1994, 1995, 1996, 2000, 2001, 2002. Used by permission of Tyndale House Publishers, Inc.

DEDICATION

To my mentor, friend, and former pastor Joe Sarver, who went home to Jesus in 2004.

The first day I walked into Joe's church, the Lord said, *This is my man Joe. Sit under him and learn.*

I did.

TABLE OF CONTENTS

Acknowledgments 7
Introduction 9
Preparation 11
   First Step: Recognize Your Responsibility 11
   Second Step: Resolve to Act 16
   Third Step: Determine Your Goal 21
   Fourth and Final Step: Assess and Plan 25
Basic Training: Maintain Your Foundation 29
   Part One: The Bible—Knowing the Truth 29
   Part Two: Repentance—Willingness to Change 36
Transformation: Learn His Voice and His Ways 47
   Area One—From Feelings to Following: What am I Feeding? (Lust of the Flesh) 51
   Area Two—From All-About-Me to "I AM": Who's in Charge? (Pride of Life) 57
   Area Three—From Taking to Thanksgiving: Where is my Focus? (Lust of the Eyes) 66
Testimony: My Journey to the Starting Line 73
Testimony: If I Can, So Can You 79
Final Challenge 99
Meet The Author 103

ACKNOWLEDGMENTS

THANK YOU, Don, for your unconditional love and support. You allowed me to quit my job to pursue my dream to write and then patiently waited four years for me to get started. You've always loved me and believed in me, even when I made it very difficult for you to do so.

Thank you, Mom and Dad, Lenne', and Robin for your time to read my drafts and give your thoughts and edits. Your positive feedback about what you read sparked excitement in me to complete the book and to believe this could actually happen.

Thank you, Chris A., for your persistent questioning. I knew that every time I saw you, you'd ask, "How's the book coming? Have you been working on it?" God spoke through you to remind me that I indeed had an assignment and that I'd better get to it. You encouraged me more than you realize.

Thank you to my friends and family – without each and every one of you, I'd not be who I am today. And I'd not have so many experiences to write about (smile).

Thank you to my spiritual mentors who loved me, prayed for and with me, guided me, and most of all, who weren't afraid to correct me when I needed it.

Thank you to Charles Stanley and Joyce Meyer for presenting the Word of God directly and with passion. Your teachings have been and continue to be foundational and inspiring.

Thank you, Athena, for taking time to listen to my idea and then encouraging me that it was worth pursuing.

Thank you, Eva Marie, Susan, and my awesome critique group for your edits.

And most of all, thank you, Jesus, for all You are to me and all You've done in me and through me. You are amazing! I'm honored and blessed beyond words that You have entrusted me with this opportunity. May these words bring You honor and glory.

1

INTRODUCTION

AS CHRISTIANS, we are called to grow and maintain an active, daily relationship with Jesus: to "work out our salvation with fear and trembling" (Philippians 2:12).

How do we do that? Let me tell you a little bit about what I learned and why I wrote this book.

Since I dedicated my life to Jesus at an older age (I was 35), I had to unlearn many behaviors adapted from living in a very ungodly world and then re-learn God's ways. Many of the world's ways are centered on us and what we can do for ourselves. God's way is the way of love and is based upon what we can do for others. Each day, I can choose to invest time knowing God more by reading His word and spending time with Him or do what I feel like doing and plop myself in front of the TV. I can choose to accept and be thankful for what I have and focus on what I could give to others or complain about what God hasn't done yet for me or how life is so unfair. I can choose to obey something God has clearly told me to do or choose to do what I want.

I realized that living for God was not about "giving up," but about exchanging. Everything in life has a price. Buying an item at the store costs money; and if you don't pay the price, the cost is you don't get the item. Losing weight and gaining health cost time and discipline; but if you don't do it, the cost is you continue to feel lousy, clothes don't fit, you take on health risks, etc. The same is true for spiritual peace. The cost of clinging to your old ways is that you'll never discover the peace, joy, and fullness of life that only God can provide. If you are willing to pay the price to give up old ways, you not only gain increased peace and joy, but you can also reveal Jesus to others by your life example, just like those who revealed Jesus to me.

My hope through this book is to share some of what I've learned in order to encourage you. If I can do it, so can you! Jesus died to make it possible for us to live as we were created to live: to the full (John 10:10). When we do so, God's love is revealed, and the Kingdom of God advances so that many will come to the saving knowledge of Jesus Christ.

And *that* is what life is all about.

2

PREPARATION

First Step: Recognize Your Responsibility

NEVER BEFORE has there been such a mentality of entitlement. Personal responsibility and accountability are viewed as archaic. Many are living under a victim mentality that excuses them from having to be responsible for their lives: their place in life, their actions, their health, and most of all, their choices.

Twice in John (5:1-14 and 8:1-11), Jesus says, "Go and sin no more." He heals and then expects those He heals to change something about their lives so they will not get to that sinful place again. It is not a request on His part; it is a command, and Jesus never commands us to do that which we are unable to do.

I've heard people say, "I can't help it; if there's food in the house, I'll eat it." Or, "But you don't know what I've been through …" or "If you had to live with him/her, you'd drink too!" Behind each statement is the foundational belief that their actions are not their fault. In each case, they have proudly made themselves victims of something outside their control.

I myself have tried to skirt responsibility with statements like, "But if they didn't say _____, I wouldn't have been *forced* to say _____," or "It's just the way I am." Truth is, those statements are just excuses: ways to justify in our minds the poor choices we are making. Instead of rising and declaring, "I can do this," we hide behind self-defeating statements that will keep us where we are. It is no different than someone who says, "I just can't seem to lose weight and get in shape," as they stuff another brownie in their mouth while sitting on the couch watching TV. We'd all see the futility in that, and can easily see that they are choosing to stay where they are. But of course, *our* situation is always different.

Our society has glamorized being a victim and, thus, encourages us to blame someone or something else for our actions and choices. Instead of facing consequences, those who commit crimes and break the law are excused as victims of hard and abusive lives. Instead of seeking justice and being glad when justice is given, we are seduced into feeling sorry for them. After all, "they can't help it."

Or can they?

I might have been abused, but it's my choice to continue to abuse others. I might have developed bad habits with my health, my words, or my attitude; but when right actions are revealed to me, it's my choice to continue the bad habits in my life instead of making a change. We hear wonderful stories of how people have risen out of amazingly hard circumstances and made something of their lives. What makes these people different? I believe it is simply their resolve to take responsibility for their lives and make the required choices and sacrifices to succeed. They have no more opportunity, and in many cases, much less opportunity than most others. They earn success because of what they do with what they have.

So let me ask you, are there areas in your life you've allowed yourself to live as a victim? Have you abdicated responsibility for your actions?

Without the decision to change, you can read books like this one, ask for prayer, and plan all you want—but your efforts will only lead to frustration. God will continue to pursue and encourage you, but the action remains yours to take. No one can force change on you.

If you are ready to deal honestly with those victim areas and take responsibility for your own spiritual health and growth, keep reading. Hopefully you'll be encouraged and blessed.

Maybe you still find yourself struggling with excuses on why you *can't* do this wandering through your mind. Or maybe you can't see how change is possible but you'd like to change if you could. If that's you, I encourage you to keep reading and ask the Lord to speak to you where you need it most. Yes, you *can* do this.

God loves all of us, and it's because of His great love that He gave us free will. We can choose to make excuses for why our lives aren't what we want them to be and remain unchanged, or we can choose to take responsibility for making our lives better. Each of us has the opportunity to change, we just need to get up and take action.

I hope that's you—that you *want* to change.

But if not, if you are content to stay where you are—clinging to your old thoughts, ways, and excuses—and you are not even willing to try, stop reading now and give this book to someone else.

Challenge Questions:

1) In what area of your life would you most like to see a change?

2) Do you believe change in that area is possible?

3) What are some reasons/excuses you've made for why you are the way you are in that area?

4) Are you willing to take full responsibility for doing whatever it takes to change?

Second Step: Resolve to Act

Have you ever made up your mind to start an exercise program? You join the gym and the staff leads you on a tour of the exciting new world of shiny equipment that will transform your body in just a few short months. Your eyes light up and you set your mind saying, "This time it *will* work. I *will* come to the gym. I *will* make the time." For the first few weeks, all is going well. You are motivated to make your schedule work, and nothing stands in your way.

Then it starts to get a little old—same time, same routine, same equipment. What was once shiny and new becomes bothersome and mundane. Concurrently, the busyness of life sets in. Kids need rides to soccer practice, help with their homework. And well, they need to eat.

The "special project" at work requires you to work overtime. You miss one day at the gym, but you vow that you'll get back at it the next time. Then a friend calls and says, "Let's go do something fun," or one of the kids gets sick and needs your attention. Before you know it, you've missed several weeks and your resolve is completely eaten away. The underlying guilt turns into complete apathy. Who cares anyway?

Been there, done that, have a closet full of t-shirts! I can't tell you how many different gyms, programs and workout centers I've joined and how much home equipment I've cycled through over the past 20 years. In fact, some of it is still collecting dust in my living room! Each time I started, my resolve gave me the motivation to make time in my schedule. And each time, I enjoyed tangible results like increased energy and decreased weight—for a while.

But also each time, the infamous "something" caused me to fall away and lapse back into my fitness-less life. I know that I know that I know that I need to be working out—and I know there has to be something that will work.

I've tried aerobics classes, walking with a friend, and even a personal trainer. These solutions all worked better than exercising alone because I had someone waiting for me and expecting me to show up.

But even then, the classes ended, friends moved or their schedule changed, and the training sessions ended (unless you have unlimited funding, which I didn't). Once again it was back to just me, alone, responsible for making the required changes. I seldom succeeded past the struggle because it's easier to sit back and do nothing than to make the effort to change.

So what is the solution? Where can I find endless motivation?

What I really need is someone to do the exercising for me. Wouldn't it be awesome if we could make the choice to be fit and then it would just happen? Of course, that's silly. Imagine saying, "Hey, my friends Jenny and Kathleen are helping me out. They are going to the gym for me so I can lose weight." You'd laugh and ask me, "What planet are you living on?"

We all know that no one else can exercise or eat right for us. It really is up to us. In fact, if someone tells us they intend to lose weight and bulk up but have no plans to exercise, we'd question their sanity.

As I sit back laughing, yet remaining unchanged, what is the difference between me and those who find the time for fitness and will work it into their schedules, no matter what obstacles they face?

Simple. They've made a decision with resolve that they are the only ones who can change their own lives. Then they make a plan and discipline themselves to follow through. They are intentional in their effort to be healthy, and they reap the benefits in quality of life. Even when they must temporarily take a break due to life's circumstances, or miss a time or two of working out, or enjoy a slice of cheesecake, they don't let that sidetrack them for long. Life for them is missing something *without* exercise. Most of us easily do steps one and two (make a decision and a plan), but often fall short on step three (discipline to follow the plan). Therefore, we don't reap the benefits.

Like physical fitness, the same is true for becoming spiritually fit. We must first make the decision that we want and need to be spiritually fit and closer to God. We must decide that we want to live our lives *His* way and not our own. We must decide that bringing the Kingdom of God to this earth is the meaning of our life. We must train ourselves and our beliefs (and remember no one else can do it for us) through practice, changing habits, and retraining how we think.

And just like improvements to your physical body when you exercise, making those changes requires investing time and effort in knowing God and understanding what it means to be spiritually fit.

But before we can define specific actions, we need to look at the goal.

Challenge Questions:

1) What people, places, or things most weaken your resolve?

2) What people, places, or things most support you and help to strengthen your resolve?

3) Based on your answers, what changes do you need to make in your life?

Third Step: Determine Your Goal

In addition to our lack of resolve, another reason fitness plans often fail is that we have either unrealistic or faulty goals. For example, let's say we have been lazy and unfit for 10 years, yet we expect to run a marathon within a month. Or, we have a goal to "look like Joe/Jane"—someone who is naturally slender when our bodies are not, no matter the amount of exercise and nutritional eating. Or, most dangerous of all, we just want to be smaller so we starve ourselves and run after quick fixes to obtain a look that is fleeting at best. We want the approval of others, and looking good often gets us that approval.

Instead of these superficial goals, our goal with fitness should be overall health and well-being, to be the best we can be regardless of what that may look like on the outside. When we are properly focused, our slimming waistline and how well we feel will be natural by-products of better overall health. Any gains achieved by confusing the goal with the by-products are short-lived and will ultimately fail.

Spiritually speaking, we also set ourselves up for failure with the wrong goal. We desire to look good on the outside instead of allowing God to really change us on the inside. We set goals to act and look godlier so others will approve and accept us, or we desire to know more about God so we can make decisions we think He would make without needing to depend on Him. Once again, we are focused on ourselves. Instead, our goal should be to *love* God, *obey* Him, and *trust* Him with all that we are, all that we have, and all that we do *so that* we can truly love others. When that is our goal, we will naturally become more like Him on the inside where it counts, and our decisions will become naturally more like His decisions. When we confuse the goal with the by-product, we become judgmental and angry; and, worse yet, we remain unchanged.

After 20-plus years of walking with God, my goal is to continue moving toward loving my Lord and Savior, and to reflect that love by obeying His commands by the power of His Holy Spirit. My goal is *not* performing His commands in my own power to earn His love and approval. My logical, analytical mind wants to make sense of a concept that only my Spirit can understand.

There was a time when I had no joy as a Christian, and I was totally worn out from trying to do everything I read in the New Testament—be kind, gentle, patient, loving, and holy as He is holy, etc. But only when I continually give up my own fleshly efforts am I able to walk in His love and experience His peace and joy. We must remember the truth that right standing with God comes only through Jesus, not through our actions. Then the doing becomes natural, as it is an extension of our spiritual selves that is guided every moment by the Holy Spirit, flowing from a life lived in simple obedience.

So I ask you now, what is your goal for wanting to become spiritually fit? Is it so that you can look good or become God over areas of your life? Or is it so that you can better love and serve God; and, therefore, love and serve your family, friends, and co-workers? Becoming godlier in character is a by-product of a life lived in obedience to Him, but acting godly to appear godly should never become our goal.

Challenge Questions:

1) In what area(s) do you most "perform" for the acceptance or approval of others?

2) What has resulted from your "performance"? Do you have more peace and the approval you were seeking, or are you driven to perform even more?

3) In one statement, write your goal for becoming more spiritually fit. Be specific.

Fourth and Final Step: Assess and Plan

Hopefully, by now, you have
- recognized you are responsible for your own spiritual health,
- accepted that responsibility,
- resolved to act, and
- set the right goal.

But you may also be thinking, "Hey, I'm doing pretty well—God and I are in good standing, my prayer life is disciplined, my family is awesome, and my ministry is thriving."

Great! But are you *there* yet? I've included a few true/false questions to help you assess.

1) I always remember to pray for every need of my friends and family.
2) I never take offense when someone hurts me.
3) I always ask the Lord before making decisions.
4) I never lie, gossip, or hurt anyone with my words.
5) I always make the right choices with my time, money, and relationships.
6) I never disobey what God tells me to do.
7) I always treat others as I want to be treated.

So, what do you think?
Are you still sure you're doing okay?
Me either!

We *all* need to continue to change and be changed. No exceptions. So let's look at making a plan to reach your goal.

With physical fitness, everyone has a different starting point and different needs to remain healthy. For some, physical fitness is/was passed down from their parents. Others make changes after they become adults. No two people are alike when it comes to what it takes to be a certain size or to have a certain level of fitness. The factors and variety of choices fill many bookshelves and libraries.

So how is it possible to come up with a program that will fit every need? It's not, but there are definitely components of good health that can be applied across the board: eat the right food, exercise, drink water, and get enough sleep. Fitness should be continuously monitored, including watching your weight and getting annual checkups. Each person is responsible for learning, and then applying what they've learned, in a way that works *for them*. This takes both discipline and motivation.

Spiritually it's the same, and even magnified. The goal is to become more loving and fruitful in your life, but no two people were created alike—each one has a unique combination of gifts, abilities, and personality traits. Compound that with the different ways each person was raised and where they are in their lives right now, and it's easy to see that everyone's plan will look different.

Like a physical fitness plan, a good spiritual fitness plan will have common basic components. These components include Bible study, time with other believers who can both encourage and correct you (and aren't afraid to do so when needed), time alone with the Lord, worship, attending a good church, and continued honest assessment of your words and actions toward yourself and others.

When making your plan, first spend some time with God to get His direction. He knows your schedule and your needs. Then start with a realistic plan that you can consistently keep. For example, 10 minutes of reading the Bible every day may be easier to adjust to than finding time for 1 hour of reading every week. And if you have to be at work by 7:00 a.m. and mornings are not your best time of day, it may be better to schedule your Bible reading for later in the day. While it may be beneficial to have a weekly Bible study or worship time, nothing can substitute for daily "God time" in your schedule.

Challenge Questions:

1) Which components (reading the Bible, attending church, etc.) do you have most difficulty devoting time to on a regular basis? Why do you think they are difficult?

2) What is the impact to your relationship with the Lord as a result?

3) What immediate change can you make in your life to incorporate at least one of the components you are missing?

3

BASIC TRAINING: MAINTAIN YOUR FOUNDATION

Part One: The Bible—Knowing the Truth

KEY TO THE SUCCESS of every fitness plan is the equipment used for the workout. Spiritually, that equipment starts with the Word of God, the Bible.

God has written us a love story about His great love for us, culminating in the sacrifice of His son Jesus so that we can spend eternity with Him. The Bible is full of stories about real people with real problems and sometimes horrible sinfulness and pride. Time and again, God rescued them when they cried out to Him for help, even when they didn't deserve it. The Bible also includes stories about people who were disciplined and suffered lifelong consequences because of their choices, also out of God's great love and mercy.

In these stories, God reveals Himself, His character, and His ways. He is consistent, perfect in love and holiness, never changing, slow to anger, and rich in mercy. He is I AM, Healer, Provider, Deliverer, Alpha and Omega, Beginning and End, Love, Truth, and Light. As Jesus, He is Savior and Redeemer. As the Holy Spirit, He is Counselor and Helper. His wisdom and justice are incomparable to anyone or anything. Yet with all He reveals about Himself in His word, we will never come close to fully understanding Who He is in all of His glory. The more I learn about Him, the more I realize how little I know in comparison to all that He is. And yet as He becomes magnified to me (and so much larger than I ever imagined), I rest more securely in knowing that a truly Almighty and Sovereign God is my Father.

When we don't know what God's word says about Him, we often view Him through filters based on how our earthly fathers treated us, or based on what others say about Him. We tend to fear Him, judge Him, and think of Him as "way up there" and, therefore, not concerned about us. Instead of running into His outstretched arms to receive His love and help, we shrink away from Him in fear of judgment and condemnation. Instead of trusting and obeying Him, we make our own plans and go our own way.

His love story also includes an abundance of words of truth about us and about how God sees us. His Word says we are His beloved, His creation, His children; and we are acceptable in His sight. The way He made us is good. The way we behave may not always be good; but inside where our identity lies, we are good because we are His, and He has given us the righteousness of Jesus in exchange for our sin. We are new creations (2 Corinthians 5:17). He loves us with an everlasting love, and nothing can separate us from that love (Romans 8:37-39). We then love because He first loved us, and only because He first loved us (1 John 4:19).

When we don't know what His Word says about us, we tend to compare ourselves to others, leading to either judgment of them when they don't measure up or envy because we perceive them as being better than us. We fruitlessly try to change ourselves to what we think we should be, again with the wrong goal to look good on the outside. We live in condemnation, beating ourselves up every time we make a mistake. We strive and strain to *become* instead of resting in the truth of His Word that we already *are.*

We need to allow the truth of the Bible to define God and to define us—not the opinion of others, our experiences, our jobs, our families, our possessions, or our position in life. Only then can we begin to rely on His grace and mercy. Then in true humility, we can allow Him to change us, and we'll begin to see others through His eyes.

Reading the Bible also helps us recognize God's voice when He speaks to us. When we hear something and we're not sure if it's God or not, we can test it by whether the Bible confirms or contradicts what we've heard. While we may not always get an absolute confirmation, we know that if we find a contradiction, then what we've heard is not the truth and therefore it was not spoken by God. For example, the Bible says that God is love and that He loves us with an everlasting love. So if we hear "God could never love you" or "You'll never be good enough for God's love," we know we've heard a lie.

While not necessary, it's helpful to invest in a study Bible with notes, application sections, and a concordance (verse search by key word) in a translation you can understand. The websites www.Biblegateway.com, www.Crosswalk.com, and https://bible.org/ contain a wealth of study helps, including tools that function like a concordance. The great value of a word-search concordance is that it allows you to search for verses that contain specific words. For example, if you want to study about "mercy," looking up "mercy" in the concordance will identify relevant verses.

"God's word is living and active. Sharper than any double-edged sword, it penetrates even to dividing soul and spirit, joints and marrow; it judges the thoughts and attitudes of the heart" (Hebrews 4:12).

"All Scripture is God-breathed and is useful for teaching, rebuking, correcting and training in righteousness, so that the man of God may be thoroughly equipped for every good work" (2 Timothy 3:16-17).

"If you hold to my teaching, you are really my disciples. Then you will know the truth, and the truth will set you free" (John 8:31b-32).

Reading the Bible isn't just one of those "checklist things to do." And the purpose of reading the Bible is not to just know *about* God and fill up with intellectual knowledge or to be able to know the "rules" so we can live by following some type of formula. Rather, it is a way of getting to know who God is, how He thinks, and what He has to say about us and our place in the world *so that* we can live as God created us to live every day, in the fullness of relationship with Him. Without reading the Bible with that intent, we cannot know God, period.

Challenge Questions:

1) How often do you read the Bible and for how long each time?

2) Have you read the entire Bible at least once? If not, make a plan to do so over the next year.

3) Ask the Lord to show you what words of truth He speaks about Himself that you don't quite believe.

4) Ask the Lord to show you words of truth He speaks about you that you don't quite believe.

5) For the words in #3 and #4 above, use a concordance or other similar word search tool to look up verses that contain those words. Meditate on those verses.

Suggestion: Whenever you look up Scriptures for reference or study, write down a few verses that minister to you. Tape them on mirrors, the refrigerator, or other places in your home, office, and car where you will be frequently reminded of His truth. You can then swap them out as you move through seasons of learning.

Part Two: Repentance—Willingness to Change

In Matthew 3:8, Jesus instructs us to "prove by the way you live that you have really turned from your sins and turned to God" (New Living Translation); to "produce fruit in keeping with repentance" (NIV). Many times, we mess up in the same area over and over again. We confess that we're sorry. And then we fall again and can't understand why we don't do better. Often, it's because our repentance stops with our apology.

While we usually do feel bad about what we've done and we really want to try to do better, that's not enough. We try, but we really don't believe we can do it. So, when we fall, we get up; but we don't stand firm—we droop our shoulders and resign ourselves to "oh well, maybe I will do better next time." Then, of course, we fall again at the slightest nudge or obstacle. We're sorry, but nothing changes. Our eyes are fixed on ourselves and our weakness. This self-focused attitude gives the enemy a foothold to keep us under condemnation.

You can read the Bible all day long; but without true repentance, the words are empty. Many people want to live the Christian life, but are unsuccessful because they either don't understand repentance or are not willing to do what is required. They say, "I believe Jesus died on the cross for my sins," but they never change—their daily lives and character show little evidence of that belief.

So what is true repentance?

The dictionary definition of "repent" is "to be sorry, be remorseful, and regret what you've done." Overall, repentance requires being remorseful about what you did. Biblical repentance goes a step further than this dictionary definition. According to Easton's 1897 Bible Dictionary, evangelical repentance consists of

1) a true sense of one's own guilt and sinfulness;
2) an apprehension of God's mercy in Christ;

3) an actual hatred of sin (Ps. 119:128; Job 42:5, 6; 2 Cor. 7:10) and turning from it to God; and
4) a persistent endeavor after a holy life in a walking with God in the way of his commandments.

In other words, we must not only be sorry, but we must also turn from our ways and go in a whole new direction. Once we become Christians, the old has passed away and we are new creations in Christ (2 Corinthians 5:17). Our identity has been changed, and our lives should continually grow and change to reflect that new identity. We must continually exchange our ways for God's ways.

True repentance means taking a firm stand against sin and moving resolutely in the opposite direction from sin—shoulders back and head up, looking at Jesus. When we brace ourselves with feet firmly planted on the Rock, we send notice to our enemy that we will not bend, we will not break, and we will not give in. We choose to believe and to act on the belief that we can indeed do all things through Christ who strengthens us (Philippians 4:13). We fix our eyes on Jesus and let His glory, love, power, and grace be magnified so that all else becomes dim. We can only be transformed to ever-increasing glory (2 Corinthians 3:18) if we are continually moving in ever-increasing repentance in more areas and to greater degrees in our lives.

To help with understanding what repentance requires and what can often get in the way for all of us, I've used the word "repent" as an acronym to share what I've learned (and what I'm still learning!).

R – REALIZE that you've sinned. Be willing to admit not just that you've made a mistake, but that you've sinned. Stop justifying. Call sin exactly what it is—sin. The Lord once impressed upon me the following truth: "If you don't call it sin, you can't take it to the cross." The cross has no power over rationalizing or justifying what we've done because we're not fully acknowledging that we've sinned. We need to ask the Lord to show us His perspective on what we've done—to see how our words or behavior have hurt Him and/or hurt the person against whom we've sinned. With His help, we need to identify the sin we've committed. Have we failed to love? Have we spoken hurtful words of gossip or slander or judgment? Have we acted out of greed or envy? Or have we realized we've sinned but then tried to cover it up?

The word "sin" often causes people to cringe and then try to justify themselves. Even though sin is referenced all through the Bible, along with every person's propensity toward sin, too many times we cannot accept that the "everyone" includes us. So when we sin, we rationalize and reason and make excuses rather than admit that we've sinned.

But the Bible makes it clear that we need to confess sin to be forgiven. Proverbs 28:13 states, "He who conceals his sins does not prosper, but whoever confesses and renounces them finds mercy." 1 John 1:9 states, "If we confess our sins, he is faithful and just and will forgive us our sins and purify us from all unrighteousness." If we haven't done a wrong, what is there to forgive? We block the flow of grace and mercy into our lives by trying to cover up our sin with excuses like, "It's not that bad," or "Is it really wrong to do that?" or "I know it was wrong, but...." With these justifications, we deny the value and power of the Cross.

Why? Because we put our identity in the sin, or even the lack of sin, instead of in who we are in Christ and in who we are according to God's word. We don't understand how to balance the seemingly conflicting truths that we are all unworthy to receive God's love, yet we are so valuable and loved by God that Jesus died for us. Because we don't understand, we think that our behavior, right or wrong, is influencing God's love for us; therefore, we can't admit sin because then God wouldn't be able to love us. We stay trapped, condemned, and hopeless instead of walking in the love of the Father that is already there for us.

E – EMBRACE responsibility for what you've done. How many times do we get the first part right and call it sin, but then continue on to say how it's not really our fault? To fully experience forgiveness and for the Cross to be effective, we must be willing to accept full responsibility for our actions. Are there sometimes outside factors? Yes. But it's always our choice to allow them to influence us or to blame them (or another person) for why we did what we did.

A typical example of this is being late for an appointment with someone. Being late in and of itself may not be a sin, but the result of being late is that we disrespect the other person by not valuing their time. Yes, sometimes we may be late due to a traffic jam that's not our fault, but are we sorry we're late for how it affected the other person, or do we just throw that in as part of the explanation? I am definitely a work in progress in this area—I am often running behind schedule for one reason or another. For example, when I plan to meet someone at 8:30 and that means I need to leave my house at 8AM, I may fiddle and putter and tidy up here and there right up until 7:50, and *then* get in the shower when I suddenly realize the time. It is a selfish mindset to not be conscious of the time; therefore, I am violating the simple law of love. My apology goes something like this, "So sorry I'm late, but I got distracted with stuff around the house." It's humbling to realize as I write this that I'm often just spitting out the words I've been trained to say, expecting understanding and forgiveness. I'm not really sorry at all.

It's especially hard for me to embrace responsibility for my own sin when what I say or do is in reaction to someone else's sinful behavior. For example, when someone else treats me wrongfully, my natural reaction is to respond in kind. Can you relate? Fortunately, I have a very wise and loving friend who is not afraid to tell me, "Yes, I know he/she hurt you and I'm sorry, but how did you respond?" She correctly points out (and has done so many times) that it doesn't matter what anyone else says or does. My only responsibility is for my own words and actions. Another person's sin can never be an excuse for me to sin in return.

Other ways we justify are by saying things like:
- "Sorry I reacted angrily, but that's a weak spot in me that the Lord is working on."
- "Sorry I forgot your birthday, but I've just been so busy lately."
- "Sorry I hurt you, but _____ (fill in the blank)."

My sister-in-law once told me that she realized saying "sorry, but" totally invalidated the apology. We're not really sorry; instead, we're explaining why we messed up—justifying what we did and then trying to sell it to the other person so they are not mad at or disappointed with us. Our concern is not really about them, but about ourselves and how we look to them.

P – PRAY. Pray to ask for forgiveness, pray to bless the other person, pray for God's mercy and grace to cover your sin. Pray to forgive yourself. Get alone with God and take it all to Him, being completely honest with Him and with yourself—He knows it anyway. Then choose to speak words of life. Receive by faith His forgiveness, His love, and His peace.

In the case of someone else's wrong triggering a sinful response in you, you also need to pray to forgive them and bless them. When you do, the Lord can work in their life in ways you cannot, no matter what you say or do.

Most of all, pray for God's grace to enable you to stay on the right path. Sadly, sins can become bad habits and, as such, need to be broken. Pray for the Lord to soften your conscience in that area and for Him to quickly and firmly convict you when you step off the path.

This continues to be an area of struggle for me and a big waste of time. Often my prayers start with all the excuses as to why I acted in the way I did, then move on to how it was not really my fault, and then eventually end with my admittance of guilt and request for forgiveness. I also plot and plan how I am going to "fix" everything and make it right. This is wrong. While I need to accept responsibility for my sin and, sometimes, make retribution, I don't need to "pay" for what I've done. Neither do you nor does anyone. Jesus already did that.

E – EXPECT consequences to continue. We may be forgiven and truly changed, but the effects of our sinful actions often linger. We find this surprising and often take offense when we're misunderstood, or when someone doesn't immediately respond in ways we think they should. If we break someone's trust by sharing something told to us in confidence, that person may not be willing to share anything else confidential. If we judge someone and act toward someone out of that judgment, he or she may not want to be around us or may not speak warmly toward us. If we lie to someone, that person may not readily believe what we say the next time.

Most recently, I've experienced this with my husband, Don. The Lord has been continually working on my heart in the areas of how I judge him and how I show (or don't show) him respect with my words. Often the disrespect and judgment are reflected in *how* I say the words rather than in the specific words themselves. As the Lord has been changing my heart, my behavior has reflected more respect and admiration for Don. While he immediately noticed the change, he also continued to react to certain words or phrases even though the intent and tone behind them was totally different. For example, "Can you please turn down the TV?" evoked the response, "Yes, boss," because previously my tone made those seven words sound like, "I can't believe you're even watching TV. I can't stand the TV. Why do you have to watch it at all, let alone have it so loud?" I felt the change on the inside and knew I had just made a simple request, but when Don heard those words, they still triggered the old response. At first, I became defensive and many arguments ensued; but because I had truly repented and God had changed my heart, eventually Don's reactions mirrored the way the words were spoken.

N – NO MORE! The enemy will continue to tempt us where we have repented, especially where our sins turned into bad habits. Old habits are hard to break, like my habitually running late. I set alarms, set reminders on my phone, and resolve to get better. Still, I can't seem to get out the door on time.

Another difficult-to-break and all-too-common habit is gossip. Someone may be convicted of gossiping and resolve to stop. Then they don't necessarily *repeat stories* but find themselves speaking negatively about someone else.

When the Lord brings conviction and correction, we must resolve to respond to His nudge and take action immediately, firmly, and *completely*. Someone once told me that being mostly obedient is still disobedience. We must be willing to do whatever it takes to continue to walk in our new, changed way.

One area in my life that gets a good workout here is judgmental thoughts. As I waited to have my nails done one day, I noticed a young girl sitting next to me with a blood red French manicure. (With a French manicure the tips of the nails are traditionally white; hers were red.) With a swift look at her, I saw that she wore her hair in her eyes, heavy make-up, and tight clothes. In my mind, this stereotyped her as a rebellious teenager. The man doing her nails had similar thoughts as evidenced by his conversation with her about dating. He talked to her about love and asked her what she thought it was. Much to my surprise and humiliation she said, "I believe what the Bible says about love—that's my guideline." I then looked more closely at her and noticed how sweetly she smiled and saw that her clothes were not *that* revealing. In fact, she simply dressed as a typical teenager.

And I felt like the proverbial slug.

I completely failed the "no more" part of repentance. Instead of firmly saying no to the first judgmental thought that came into my mind about her nails and asking God for *His* thoughts about her, I let my resolve slip and allowed the other judgmental thoughts free entry. Thankfully, the Lord humbled me when He let me see a little bit of her heart for Him; and I was able to smile at her and offer words of encouragement.

We also need to say "No more!" to condemnation. This includes quickly asking forgiveness, forgiving ourselves when we do slip up, and getting right back on track. It's easy to quit and beat ourselves up when we make a mistake, just like it's easy to quit working out when we miss a few days. But we can't become sidetracked from our goal – we need to get up and keep going! We must focus on our secure identity in Christ, not on the mistake.

T – TELL someone about it. Light and accountability are crucial to staying on the right path. Maybe the sin is something private, like looking at pornography. We realize it is sinful, embrace responsibility (yes, I visited that website), pray for forgiveness, and expect to continue with the struggle. We even say, "No more—I will not look at this ever again!" and we mean it. But then the temptations bombard us. "Hey, no one knows, and it's right here, and…." Before we know it, we've fallen again. Condemnation and shame thrive in that darkness, and they quickly barrage us with despair and hopelessness.

Telling another person and praying with them brings light, and it also brings Jesus front and center into the picture.

> "For where two or three come together in my name, there am I with them" (Matthew 18:20).

> "Therefore confess your sins to each other and pray for each other so that you may be healed. The prayer of a righteous man is powerful and effective" (James 5:16).

> "Carry each other's burdens, and in this way you will fulfill the law of Christ" (Galatians 6:2).

We need the acceptance of someone who loves us and knows our darkness and the power of standing two together.

Challenge Questions:

1) With what area of repentance (which letter) do you most struggle? Write down a few examples of your struggles.

2) What have you done or said recently that requires an apology, but you've been reasoning away your actions? When are you going to go back and apologize?

3) Using use a concordance or other similar word search tool, look up verses that contain the words "repent," "mercy," "forgive." Meditate on those verses.

4

TRANSFORMATION: LEARN HIS VOICE AND HIS WAYS

WHEN WORKING OUT at the gym, it's not uncommon to have someone review all of the equipment with us and help us determine which equipment will bring the most benefit. For eating right, we may consult books and other avenues that can help us know which food will be best. In both cases, we are looking to an expert who has experience and can guide us along. If we do as they say, follow their principles and formulas, we'll enjoy physical transformation.

Spiritually, we have the Holy Spirit—the Counselor, Helper, and Guide—as our expert. We need to learn more about how to hear His voice and follow His ways. If we do as He says, we'll enjoy spiritual transformation from the inside out. Unlike physical fitness, though, following the Holy Spirit is not a listen-once-and-follow-the-formula discipline. It's a relationship. We walk with Him and converse with Him every day.

I've already mentioned that the first and foundational step is knowing His voice: reading the Bible so we can know God and what He says about us. The next step is getting things out of the way that interfere with His voice.

This chapter focuses on three primary problem areas where we can be out of balance and, therefore, unable to hear God clearly. One, we are driven by our feelings and desires; two, we want what we see, and we want it now; and three, we are in control so we don't need anyone or anything. 1 John 2:16 names these problem areas the lust of the flesh, the lust of the eyes, and the pride of life. Read each of the following translations of 1 John 2:15-16. Notice the very clear contrast between the world and the love of Jesus.

The New International Version (NIV):
Do not love the world or anything in the world. If anyone loves the world, the love of the Father is not in him. For everything in the world—the cravings of sinful man, the lust of his eyes and the boasting of what he has and does—comes not from the Father but from the world.

The Message (MSG):
Don't love the world's ways. Don't love the world's goods. Love of the world squeezes out love for the Father. Practically everything that goes on in the world—wanting your own way, wanting everything for yourself, wanting to appear important—has nothing to do with the Father. It just isolates you from him. The world and all its wanting, wanting, wanting is on the way out—but whoever does what God wants is set for eternity.

The Amplified Bible (AMP):
Do not love or cherish the world or the things that are in the world. If anyone loves the world, love for the Father is not in him. For all that is in the world—the lust of the flesh

[craving for sensual gratification] and the lust of the eyes [greedy longings of the mind] and the pride of life [assurance in one's own resources or in the stability of earthly things]—these do not come from the Father but are from the world [itself].

The New King James Version (NKJV):
Do not love the world or the things in the world. If anyone loves the world, the love of the Father is not in him. For all that is in the world—the lust of the flesh, the lust of the eyes, and the pride of life—is not of the Father but is of the world.

The New Living Translation (NLT):
Do not love this world nor the things it offers you, for when you love the world, you do not have the love of the Father in you. For the world offers only a craving for physical pleasure, a craving for everything we see, and pride in our achievements and possessions. These are not from the Father, but are from this world.

In today's world, following Jesus and living like Jesus are incredibly difficult because we are constantly striving against the victim mentality and our selfish culture of entitlement. As we've discussed already, choice is the key. We must challenge ourselves: "Am I willing to invest time feeding myself with what is pure, lovely, and excellent, and turn away from things that drain me, bring me down, and make me lazy?" As with physical exercise, spiritual discipline starts with a belief that it's both possible and necessary. After the belief, we must decide with resolve to do whatever it takes to change.

If we seriously want to follow Jesus as His disciple and lead others to Him, growing in our relationship with Him and allowing Him to transform us is not an option. It is a *necessity*.

Once we make the decision to move away from the world and be closer to Jesus, we need to identify the worldly areas of influence in our lives and then take steps toward spiritual fitness in those areas. The next sections address moving from "F.A.T." to "F.I.T.": from Feelings (lust of the flesh) to Following, from All-about-me (pride of life) to I AM, and from Taking (lust of the eyes) to Thanksgiving.

Area One—From Feelings to Following: What am I Feeding? (Lust of the Flesh)

"I don't feel like it."
"Because I felt like it."
"Because I no longer have any feelings for _____ (you, God, prayer)."
"He needs to understand how I feel!"
"I can't help myself!"
"If it feels good, do it."

Most advertising is specifically designed to appeal to the senses—tastes great, sounds awesome, or you'll feel and look younger in just weeks! Songs are filled with lyrics that glorify feelings. Movies are all about falling in and out of love and are full of choices made based on how people feel in any given moment. Consequences for choices are minimized or non-existent in the media—the characters are just victims of things around them. Add the Christian-ese statements such as "feeling the anointing" and "feeling God's presence" to those advertising techniques and we can easily be swept away by the tide of our emotional culture.

Not that feelings in and of themselves are wrong. Jesus as a man was full of emotion. But His feelings were in response to events and people around Him; His focus stayed on doing the will of His Father who was His only guide. When we focus on our feelings, giving them too much attention or allowing *them* to be our guide, we become tossed to and fro and quickly lose control. Our feelings take the throne and become our idol, and then we wonder why our lives are so unstable.

Why do we continue to let our emotions rule us? One reason is because it allows us to avoid accepting responsibility. Since we're not in control, obviously what happens is not our fault—we're just innocent victims, like the characters in the movies we watch.

"Hey, it's not my fault I'm overweight—I just can't help myself when it comes to food!"

"I really want to lose weight, but I never feel like exercising."

"I'm sorry I hurt you, but you made me angry."

So how do we de-throne our feelings? Simple. Stop feeding them everything they want. Deny them. Put off the old man, and put on the new man full of righteousness and holiness.

Closely related to our feelings is our flesh: sin, the old self, the corrupted nature. Our flesh is kept alive and kicking when we "feed" it—when we

- give in to the temptation and the old ways and make poor choices,
- keep speaking and believing the lies that we've always lived by, or
- refuse to allow God to rule over that place, shine His light, and reveal His truth.

We start to experience the death of the old fleshy self, and we say, "Oh no, part of me is going to be lost forever. I must hang on!" We block God's work in our lives.

We fail to realize the basic truth that how we were in our old self is not how we really are as a child of God. The death of the old life is the only way to experience the resurrection of the new life God has already died to give us. We must choose to feed our spirits and starve our flesh, walking in obedience to God instead of going wherever our feelings lead us.

I've met so many people who sincerely believe they are powerless to control their flesh and, for example, stop eating junk food. They have become victims of their flesh instead of overcomers by the power of the Holy Spirit. Not only does this rob them of true peace and joy and a whole host of other blessings, but it is also an insult to the Holy Spirit. What they've said, in essence, is that His power is not great enough. This is an open invitation for the enemy to bring condemnation and guilt.

So yes, starving our flesh is a matter of belief as well as a matter of choice. Whatever we believe and, therefore, dwell on has power. If we truly believe we are powerless to stop eating, we are just that. We must attack that wrong belief by investing time in knowing God's word, and allowing it to change the way we think. Then we must obey what it says no matter how we feel. We don't ignore our feelings or suppress them, but neither do we allow them to rule our choices. Instead of doing things our way, we lay down our lives, deny ourselves, pick up our cross, and follow Jesus. We obey as a choice of our will, not because we have a feeling to do this or that. This is a simple concept, although it is not always easy to put into practice because in many of us, our flesh is strong.

Last of all, we must stop the flow of feeling-oriented messages into our spirits by exchanging the time we spend feeding ourselves on emotionally-charged entertainment with time feeding on the spiritual food provided by the Bible, music that honors God, fellowship, and time alone with God. Every one of our choices will either lead us closer to Jesus or numb us to Him by causing barriers between Him and us. We need to resolve to protect what we watch, what we read, what we hear, and what we eat.

Challenge Questions:

1) Think about a time recently when you reacted hastily based on your feelings. What was the result? What could you have done differently?

2) What do you read/watch/eat/listen to that most turns you away from Jesus and toward making you feel good in your flesh?

3) What should you be eating—feeding upon—instead? (Hint – this answer is not always "the Bible")

4) What steps are needed to make that happen?

5) Are you willing?

6) Using a concordance or other similar word search tool, look up verses that contain the words "obey," "obedience," "flesh," and "temptation," focusing on New Testament verses. Meditate on those verses.

7) Using a concordance or other similar word search tool, look up verses that contain the word "feelings." Did you find any verses?

Area Two—From All-About-Me to "I AM": Who's in Charge? (Pride of Life)

> "If you don't look out for yourself, who will?"
> "God helps those who help themselves."
> "Just believe in yourself and you can do anything you want!"
> "I'm the maker of my own destiny!"
> "My life is mine—no one has the right to tell me what I can and can't do."
> "If God didn't want me to make decisions, he wouldn't have given me a brain."
> "It's my body and I can do what I want with it."

These messages of the world are designed to keep us in control and self-sufficient, pridefully depending on ourselves for everything. The results are not peace and joy but frustration and anger at ourselves and others when we can't make things happen the way we want. They don't call this sin area the "pride of life" for nothing. Instead of reading the Bible to know Jesus and trust Him more, we read it like a "how to" manual and try to follow it in our own strength and in our own way, to get something for ourselves. We don't want to depend on God; we want a formula to follow. We say, "Okay, Lord, I'm going this way, bless me," and then complain when things don't work out and God doesn't cooperate with our plan.

We avoid asking for the Lord's help or direction because deep down inside we know He won't bless selfish motives, but then we run to Him when our way of doing things fails. We may even find ourselves stubbornly stuck in this cycle because we refuse to admit our need and then give the controls fully to the Lord.

Why are we so reluctant to trust God with everything? One reason is because the world is increasingly void of any reference or mention of God or His great love for us. When we don't know someone, and we don't know that that person cares deeply for us, we find it difficult to trust that person. If we neither trust nor believe that person has our best interests at heart, what motivation do we have to obey and follow him? The same is true for God. We don't trust Him because we don't know Him.

Knowledge of and trust in God's voice and His love for us is not something that happens in a one-time encounter. We know God's voice and learn to trust Him because of a day-by-day choice to involve God in all that we say and do. Again, we must read His Word continually to know how much He treasures and values us; and we must step out in the faith we have already attained. I am a definite work-in-progress with absorbing how much He loves me into every fiber of my being.

The stepping-out-in-faith part is an area of my life where I have failed and continue to fail in little ways and in big ways. As I mentioned, I am blessed/cursed with an extremely analytical and logical mind. Because of this, I tend to lean on my own understanding, which hinders both my ability to hear God and my desire to stop and ask Him for direction. Many times I've been leaving the house and have had a random thought, *Take such-and-such with you*. Almost immediately, my own next thought came, *No, I won't need that*. Instead, I should have stopped to ask, *Lord, is that You?* Later, the need for what I didn't bring comes to light, along with that random thought that I dismissed. I can only admit, *Oh, that* was *you, Lord,* and then either go back to get the item, or make do without it. God was trying to make my life easier as He so delights in doing, and I missed it.

Another way we take control, and often don't even see it, is to use Bible verses to infer direction from the Lord that He is not providing. Yes, even the Bible can become a substitute for the Lord when it's not His direction that takes us there, or when we are reading with the wrong intent.

Many years ago I dated a man whom I thought the Lord brought into my life to marry because I had recently felt "led" to read verses about marriage and children and from that inferred that he was "the one." But all the Lord had directly told me was to "love him, accept him, and speak the truth to him." Instead of seeking godly counsel for confirmation (sometimes God speaks through others more clearly than we can hear on our own, especially concerning matters of the heart), I decided to avoid my friends altogether. I kept dating this man. As a result, we were both hurt when things didn't work out between us. In fact, God had to move me 700 miles away to another state to completely end the relationship.

I've also had some success stories. I wanted to buy a Bible for a friend, and I kept being drawn to a King James Version translation. Since I find that version hard to read, I couldn't see how the Lord could possibly want me to get that one for my friend. But, I also couldn't argue with the peace I had when I picked up that particular Bible. So I bought it and gave it to my friend. She loved it and told me how she thought the "language was just so beautiful."

Another time was when my husband Don first became a Christian. He wanted some Christian music, so I compiled a music cassette for him. (If you don't know what a cassette is, ask someone who was born before 1980.) He and I both liked rock style music, but the only songs I had peace about were soft, slow-tempo worship songs. So I made the cassette with the slow songs and gave it to him. He talked for months about how the music helped him experience God's nearness and how God spoke to him each time he played it.

From those examples and many others, I've learned that one of the most certain indicators that we are not walking in God's will and with His guidance is when we don't have His peace—the peace that passes all understanding (Philippians 4:7). I'm not talking about a feeling, but a deep down "knowing" from the Holy Spirit that you are in complete agreement with God and with what He wants for you at that moment. You may *feel* anxious, nervous, or even a bit afraid, but deep down you know that it's what God wants you to do.

I once made plans for friends to come visit; but right before they finalized the plans, I realized I didn't have God's peace about the visit. Instead of talking to them about it, I figured that since they wanted to come, and since I wanted them to come, everything would work out. I said, "Yes, come on down!" They bought plane tickets and we made final arrangements.

The week before their visit, I found out why they were not supposed to come. It had nothing to do with them, but with circumstances in my life that changed. God knew all that would happen and had tried to show me by lack of His peace that I would not need company when those particular dates rolled around. I didn't listen. Therefore I had another choice to make: let them come anyway, or obey the Lord and tell them not to come. Fortunately I chose to obey, but the cost was high. Our friendship changed after that day, plus I had to pay for their unused airline tickets.

We are all in some state of transferring control over to the Lord, seeing how much better He does with our lives, and learning to fully know His voice. Very few people can become Christians and immediately fully know God's grace and mercy, and turn everything in their lives over to Him. I'm so envious of those who learn that early. (Oops, I mean, I'm *excited* for them!) But that's the goal – to have Him be Lord over our relationships, our finances, our time, our investments, our dreams, our desires—yes, everything!

God wants control of it all because He knows He can do so much more with our lives than we can ever do on our own. He will gladly and gently lead us toward giving it all to Him, one step at a time, if only we let Him. Without Him in the driver's seat, it is impossible to live the Christian life to the full, and thereby walk in His love and bring the Kingdom of God to those around you.

Challenge Questions:

1) Do you live as though you believe the Lord can do a better job than you can in running your life? In what specific area do you have difficulty trusting God? Why?

2) Do you pray and seek Godly counsel instead of worldly wisdom for all major decisions in your life, or do you reason and rationalize why you've made the decisions and then ask God to bless them? What decision did you make recently where you did not ask the Lord *first*, and you should have?

3) Do you ask God every day for His opinion, guidance, and direction in all things, or do you only turn to Him for the big things or when in trouble?

4) Do you believe God is good and trustworthy and faithful, or do you doubt His love for you? Why?

5) Do you say "I know God will _____ (take care of, help, provide for, etc.) me," or do you say "I know God can, but I'm not sure that He will so I need to help Him?" In what area(s) are you compelled to "help" God the most?

6) Using a concordance or other similar word search tool, look up verses that contain the words "LORD" (Old Testament), "I am" (as spoken by God or Jesus), "God is," and "faith." Meditate on those verses.

7) Read Job 38-41. (Yes, it's a long passage, and very powerful.) What did God reveal to you as you read? What specific verses spoke to you?

Area Three—From Taking to Thanksgiving: Where is my Focus? (Lust of the Eyes)

> "If you want it, go for it."
> "Life is short—take all you can get!"
> "Why wait when I can have it now?"
> "Go for the gusto!"
> "How come *they* can do it/have it and I can't?"
> "You deserve _____ (that job, vacation, new TV, etc.)—why not!"
> "They're no better than you and they have one!"

All of these messages are designed to get us to act on impulse and emotion to gain something for ourselves. This often leads us to live way beyond our means and make hasty decisions we regret later when the bill comes in. We whip out our credit cards and act fast before we lose that great deal. We reason that whatever "it" is, it is meant for us to have because we work hard and deserve to have the best. And we want it now.

Waiting on the Lord is sometimes painful, and we don't always get it our way. Again, we reason and rationalize, "What difference does it make if I do it now or wait if the Lord said I could have it?"

We also act out of competition to have what others have. Or to define ourselves by what we have. Instead of being thankful for what we have and where we are, we constantly compare our status to others and then we're motivated to act so that we measure up. We confuse abundant life and blessings with possessions. We see it, we want it; after all, we deserve it. Our focus is on what we see and how we could get it for ourselves. Sometimes even when we get what we want, we're still not happy.

One morning, the Lord drew my attention to Ecclesiastes 6:2, "God gives a man wealth, possessions and honor, so that he lacks nothing his heart desires, but God does not enable him to enjoy them, and a stranger enjoys them instead. This is meaningless, a grievous evil." I did not understand. God gave the man riches, and then God didn't allow him to enjoy them. Why not?

Maybe it's a lesson on the focus of satisfying your soul (flesh, mind, will, emotions). The man desired all of those things for his soul—he wanted to live a good life here on earth, full of earthly pleasures. But they turned out to be useless because God then did something in the man's life—maybe health issues—that didn't enable him to enjoy what he had.

Maybe it's a lesson on desiring earthly things versus eternal things. The man died and could not take any of his prize possessions with him. Plus, all possessions can be either broken, lost, or destroyed, so putting his heart too much on earthly things and building life around his things didn't bring him peace. Maybe God took away his enjoyment in an attempt to get him to change his focus.

Maybe it's a lesson on ownership. The man appears to have taken those things for his own instead of recognizing that he was just a steward—God owns it all. Instead of being thankful to God, he pridefully accumulated them as his right. He did not acknowledge that God gave him the talents and gifts he used to earn, have, and keep his possessions. While God desires to bless us with things of the world for our enjoyment, we always need to hold them loosely. And be willing to give them away as He leads us.

Whatever the full meaning, one thing is now clear to me: everything we are and all we have is a gift from God and is intended to be used for His purposes. He created everything, so He, therefore, has ownership rights over all. When we forget that and live as owners rather than as stewards, using what we have for our pleasures instead of His eternal purposes, God can take what we have and give it to someone else. Not that we can't enjoy life here on earth, but if we stop seeking the kingdom first with what we are given, we may find that all other things are taken away from us.

Sadly, for some people this principle applies to their relationships.

> "We love each other and are getting married anyway, so why wait to have sex?"
> "She makes me so happy—I can't live without her!"
> "I'm so tired of being alone and I know the Lord has said I'd have a wife/husband. I know this person may not be all I wanted, but he's/she's good enough."

We settle for what we can have now and what the world tells us is "love" instead of allowing Jesus to fulfill what He has for us in His way and in His time. Our focus is not really on the other person and what's best for them, or on God and what He'd want for us, but on ourselves and how that person can make us happy, fulfill us, or provide what we need. Often God will answer our prayer, "God, I want *Your* choice for my mate," by ending a relationship we've started. We shake our fist at Him and wonder what He's doing to us instead of being thankful that He's saved us from making a mistake.

One last and very evident manifestation of our self-centeredness and take-what's-mine mentality is our entitlement-based culture. If *you* have something I need, *I* have a right to have it. Once again the focus is on *me,* what I need, and what I have a "right" to. Or if you have it, you must give it to me. Or, if I can't find the job I want, or don't really want to work, someone else will take care of me.

We miss the Lord's best by trading in waiting on the Lord and being thankful for what He's given us for grabbing what we want now. And we miss out by taking ownership instead of recognizing it's all His anyway and allowing Him to direct how we use/spend our possessions. The result is death to our peace, destruction to the very best life He died to give us, and a slow and steady burial under all that with which the enemy wants to bombard us.

To see where you stand with ownership, do a quick inventory of your most prized possessions, including all of your relationships. Ask yourself, "What if God asked me to give 'x' away?" and see how your heart reacts. If you sincerely want to seek God's kingdom first, be ready for God to move on your behalf and remove anything or anyone in your life that is in His way. And be thankful when He does just that!

Challenge Questions:

1) Do you spend only what you have and also save for the future, or do you pretty much get what you want, when you want it, and just charge it if you don't have the money? What recent purchase did you make that you now regret?

2) Has the Lord asked you to give something away that you still own? If so, what is it? What is stopping you from doing as He asked?

3) Are you in a relationship right now that you know is not the Lord's best, but you'd rather have it than be alone? Have you talked to God about it? What did He say?

4) If you're single, are you saving yourself for your spouse? If you haven't, are you willing to start now and stay celibate until marriage?

5) Do you envy anyone of something they have that you have been waiting for? Describe.

6) Using a concordance or other similar word search tool, look up verses that contain the words "wait," "giving," "thankful," "trust." Meditate on those verses.

5

TESTIMONY: MY JOURNEY TO THE STARTING LINE

MY JOURNEY to sold-out faith in Jesus Christ was a somewhat long and analytical trip. Along the way, several key people influenced both my decision to follow Jesus and my life as a Christian. I've unlearned, learned, and re-learned many things I want to share in the hopes that the path may be made a bit easier for you.

I was raised in a wonderful family—our parents loved us dearly and we all knew that. As Catholics, we attended mass every Sunday, CCD (Sunday school) classes, and participated in all the rituals along the way. The Bible verses and stories I read and heard laid a solid foundation for my knowledge of God but did very little to help me understand how to live in a relationship with Him. I also didn't understand true salvation: salvation by faith in Christ where your identity is changed by the power of the Holy Spirit, and you live in a living, breathing, daily relationship with Jesus. I performed for God, but didn't relate to Him as Father, or to Jesus as Lord. And since faith and religion was taught to be a private thing, we seldom talked about our faith in or our relationship with God.

I am not condemning the Catholic faith in any way. I'm just relating my experience. I know many Catholics who have come to awesome saving faith in Jesus and have a wonderful relationship with Him. It just didn't happen that way for me.

Once I graduated from high school and moved out on my own, church attendance stopped except for the obligatory Easter and Christmas services. During the next 15 years, I married and divorced twice (with no children from either marriage), developed a successful career in computer analysis and programming, and achieved a Bachelor's degree in Business Administration by attending night school. While I enjoyed my successful career, and my personal life moved along after my second divorce, I knew something was missing. I felt restless and empty, so I began searching for the proverbial "meaning of life."

Then in 1990, two significant events happened that guided my quest in a spiritual direction.

First, I met one of my cousins who lived differently because of a very solid faith in Jesus, yet hanging out with her was fun. Second, my brother gave me a study Bible for my birthday. Up until that time, I thought born-again Christians were weird. Every time I ran into them, they were either smiling, pleasant, and sappy-happy or they were hypocritical, judgmental, and stern. I wanted no part of either. But my brother and my cousin were just down-to-earth, normal people like me; yet they had a peace I knew I didn't possess.

A third event that kept me on the path toward God happened the next year. I worked closely with another born-again Christian on a consulting project. She, too, had a peaceful, rock-solid faith and was 100 percent certain of what she believed. She accepted me fully as I was, even with all my warts! I can remember talking about the leap of faith I felt I needed to take. We had more than a few conversations that went something like this:

> Me: "What if it isn't true?"
> Her: "But it is!"
> Me: "What if I leap and it doesn't work?"
> Her: "But it will!"

She never once wavered or doubted. I wanted that sense of security, but I had so many questions. Having the natural-born blessing/curse of an extremely active and analytical mind, I could not jump in without knowing for sure that it was true. I also had concerns about all I'd have to "give up" if I became a Christian. Would life suddenly become boring? Would I never have any fun again?

God knows how to provide what we need instead of what we think we want. By then I was actively looking for someone who could answer all my questions so I could take a leap of faith with 100 percent certainty. Instead, He sent another strong and loving believer to me who absolutely refused to engage in any debates of any kind. At the time, she taught a class for new believers at my church. By God's divine design, I was the only one in the class so I had her undivided attention. I kept challenging her with question after question about Jesus and about Paul's letters. Her repeated, simple response (are you seeing a theme here?) was, "All God wants you to do is love Him and let Him love you." She said this to me over and over and over again.

At that time I thought Jesus was an arrogant snob. He asserted that *He* was the way, *He* was the truth, *and He* was the only one. Who did He think He was, this Jesus? And Paul's letters had so many stern "do" and "do not" commands. All I understood was the Bible putting impossible behavior goals in front of me, as dictated by this pompous Jesus and this hard-lined Paul. Then I had these women in my life who refused to defend Him or argue about His words; instead they peacefully and fully radiated His love to me.

Although I felt myself softening, I could not get past all the questions in my logical and analytical mind. Then my loving Father God played his trump card, so to speak, in May of 1992.

I was traveling from a wedding in New Jersey back to my contract job in Iowa. Picture a huge wide-body jet, 2-5-2 seating, and only one-third full at the most. I'm in a window seat, spread out for comfort with a good book; all my questions clamoring for attention, and someone has the nerve to sit next to me! I guess my look must have telegraphed my thoughts quite clearly because the man (I'll call him Rich) apologetically said, "I'll move when we get started, no problem."

Then he noticed a book I was reading, *Inside Out* by Larry Crabb. As he prepared to move, Rich looked at the book, cocked his head as though listening to someone, and then said, "Interesting book. Do you like it?" We talked a bit about it, and with that began the most amazing conversation I've ever had.

Rich was a stable, strong, loving believer on his way home from a business trip. We talked the whole trip about the book, the Bible, Jesus, God, and other areas of Christian faith, including many of my questions.

In itself, it was not an unusual conversation. We found no cure for cancer, the world's problems were left unsolved, and we did not delve into deep personal issues. What made it amazing was the delivery: Rich knew my questions, word for word, before I could ask them. As I was thinking of a question—for example, *How did they know Mary was a virgin?*—Rich would cock his head as though listening and say, "Did you ever wonder how they knew Mary was a virgin?" Then he'd proceed to either answer the question, or refer me to a verse or book that would help me discover the answer on my own.

This "mind-reading" dialogue went on for two solid hours. After the first hour, I broke down in tears and shared with him what had been happening. Tears of gratitude formed in his eyes. He had indeed been listening to the Lord's still small voice (remember how he kept cocking his head to the side) and had been hesitant to speak because the questions didn't always fit into the conversation. But he knew the Lord's voice through years of obedience and dedication to spending time with Him, so he stepped out in faith and God spoke through him in the specific way I needed to hear. I got back to my hotel in Iowa, threw myself down on the bed, and committed the rest of my life to following the Lord. I cried, "God, you win!" My walk with Jesus began.

Jesus had won my heart as only He could do. I received His gift of salvation by faith and choice—not by earning it or by my performance.

Eight months later, I moved to Illinois and attended a church which had an awesome singles' group. I began to see that a completely different culture existed. And I quickly realized that while I had received my new life by faith, I had a responsibility to invest in my relationship with God if I wanted my faith to grow. My new friends lived what they believed, didn't cuss, didn't tell dirty jokes, didn't mock people, and most of them didn't drink alcohol or smoke. We had lots of good, clean fun when we got together. I learned that you can have fun without drinking and without being physically intimate.

Since then I've been blessed and disciplined. I've fallen down and been lifted up. I have been miraculously transformed and healed of many hurts and sins from the past. I received a precious gift from the Lord of the most wonderful husband, Don, at just the right time (more about him in later chapters). I've learned—many times the hard way through failure—that the more I obey and choose God's way, the faster and more deeply He can change me. How much He changes me is directly related to my peace, joy, and contentment in life. More importantly, the more I'm changed the more loving I become with so much more to give to others. In fact, without being changed, I have nothing of value to give because I cannot give what I don't possess. While I know I've come a long way, I also realize I still have so much yet to learn and lots of growing to do.

I'm looking forward, not back, and moving closer to Jesus every day. I pray through this book I've encouraged you to do the same.

6

TESTIMONY: IF I CAN, SO CAN YOU

IN MY OWN WALK, I've found tremendous encouragement in the testimony of others. Not only from the Bible and the stories of those whose lives are shared with such brilliant color, but also of those I know and have seen gain victory over their own struggles. Testimony is powerful because no one can challenge or take away your own personal experience. Here are a few stories I hope will encourage and bless you. As many have told me, I now tell you again: If I can have "God" stories, so can you!

Right to My Front Door

Oh Lord, I am so happy being single! It's just You and me, and I don't care if we're like this forever! So if You ever want me to get married, You'll need to bring the man to my front door!

That was me on my back porch on January 20th, 2000, basking in the moonlight and enjoying God's presence. I had made the above statement about getting married tongue-in-cheek while talking to a friend a few months earlier, and I wanted to make sure the Lord had heard me.

At the time of that declaration I had been single and not dating anyone for a long time. After many years of moaning about never finding a husband, wondering what God was doing, and asking why so-and-so was getting married and I wasn't, I had finally come to a place of complete surrender and contentment with being single. At church, I was preparing to conduct a workshop titled "The Joys of Living Single: Overcoming the Barriers to Love." Friends and family were awesome, my job was good, and I had just bought a new house. Life was wonderful! Finally, I had victory in this area and had fully embraced being thankful. I truly didn't need, or even want, a husband.

Little did I know that my life was about to radically change. Actually, the change started six months earlier when my then-future husband and I bought houses across the street from each other. Due to our different schedules and lifestyles, it was almost impossible for us to meet. Over the next several months, I would learn that when we are willing to give our desires and even our hurts to God, give up our dreams for His dreams for us, and be thankful for where we are, He truly does more than we could ever ask or think. Yes, with God all things are possible; even 20 inches of snow in Raleigh, North Carolina.

On January 24th, just four days after my back porch declaration, Raleigh was *buried* under 20 inches of snow. Early that morning, I heard the scrape of snow shovels coming up my front walkway. I looked out my front window to see Don and his next-door neighbor cleaning off my sidewalk. *What gentlemen*, I thought. They shoveled all the way up to my front door. Something about Don's eyes held my attention, and with all the snow keeping us somewhat homebound, we started talking. Turns out, we had much in common. Although he didn't yet know the Lord, he had many questions and I could tell the Lord was working in his heart and life.

I could also tell the Lord was breaking me down. *Okay, Lord, did You not hear me last week?* I seemed to have traded contentment and stability for the emotions of a 16-year-old with a crush. Thankfully, I had strong roots and awesome support from my family and from friends at church. And, thankfully, I had learned from past failures that I needed them. As months went by and the friendship grew between us, by the Lord's grace, I could focus on what Don needed, which was to be rooted in God and not in a dating relationship with me.

This wasn't always easy. I spent many early mornings and late nights wrestling with God over my emotions and desires versus His will and how they didn't seem to be lining up. Before I met Don, I'd had words spoken over me about how my husband was going to be a pastor and a mighty man of God, and we were going to travel and minister together around the world. *That would be awesome*, I thought. So, I had prayed for a mature Christian, a strong man of the word, and strong leader who was already developed. My emotions were getting involved, but I could not let them rule! Don was a new Christian, one whose character and knowledge of the Word was at the infant stage. Don also kept telling me I was not his type either.

But thank God He is bigger than all of our shortcomings, insecurities, questions, and personal evaluations if only we allow Him to be God.

Our friendship continued to blossom under God's direction. Through another series of events only God could orchestrate, we became husband and wife.

But not the way I had dreamed: me in a white dress, family and friends surrounding us, big celebration afterwards. In fact, there was no planning at all. Don asked me to marry him on Sunday night, and we were married Monday morning in the church prayer room, dressed in jeans, and with only a few witnesses. Then we called our families to tell them right before leaving that afternoon on our vacation-turned-honeymoon to England and Ireland.

To this day, we've called the January 2000 snowstorm "our snow." We know the Lord brought that snow so we could meet, just like His hand guided our steps six months earlier to two houses for sale across the street from each other. I'm so thankful I didn't miss the wonderful blessing that is my marriage to Don. The cost of giving up my dreams to receive what the Lord had for me was like paying a penny for a million dollar mansion. Suffice it to say, it has been well worth it.

God had indeed brought my husband right to my front door. And He can do that for you, too.

From My Plan to His

All my life I've had a plan. It didn't matter what the situation, my logical and analytical mind could formulate a plan for it. And my plans weren't only for me; they were for everyone around me. I especially had plans for (and you wives know what's coming next) my husband!

Don and I both knew God ordained our marriage. And, with so much of our story not going according to *my* plan, it's a miracle we ever *got* married. I also knew God chose me to help Don become the man of God he was destined to be. After all, I was *so much more* of a mature Christian than Don, so my help was invaluable. I entered the marriage strong and confident in the Lord. I had been cultivating my relationship with Him for years and had first-hand experience with how He had transformed my life. It was *obviously* my duty and responsibility to pass along all I'd learned to Don for his benefit.

So once in the marriage, I took the attitude, *Okay, Lord, I can take it from here.*

Big mistake!

Pride deceived me into thinking that because of my maturity, I needed less time with the Lord. With all my godly background, I knew what was best for both Don *and* for our marriage. I gradually but steadily slid down that slope of relying less on Him and more on my own experience and strength. I tried and tried and *tried* to take control over Don's spiritual growth while ignoring my own.

The sobering truth is that if my husband were not a man so strongly devoted to God, my "help" would have ended our marriage.

During the first years of our marriage, we endured (or should I say, *Don* endured) many cycles of me trying to fix him, repenting and letting him go, experiencing peace in our house, then becoming discontented again so I'd have to fix him again. By the grace of God and my continued choices to allow God to dig deeply into areas I didn't want to see, this fix-repent-peace-discontentment cycle was finally broken. I had to be willing to see myself for the ugly, controlling, sinful woman I was and to see how others viewed my sinful pride. I remember one time when I prayed about hurtful words someone had said to Don. Without missing a beat the Lord said, "What about your words?"

My heart broke! I realized that, not only had I said hurtful words in private, but I'd also said very disrespectful words concerning him in front of others.

As I repented of my behavior I began to see God working in both of our lives. I was still reaping what I had sown through years of sin; but, thankfully, the grace of God is more powerful than my sin.

I am blessed beyond measure with God's choice for me in Don. While he may not have a formal seminary degree, God brought me a man with a heart after God, like David, and an inner strength, wisdom, and gentleness that is exactly what I need. What Don brings to my life is more than I could have ever asked or imagined. We've also had some very rough times, and both agree that only our individual relationships with the Lord kept us together through those times. Our growth together as one in marriage, and what the Lord has been able to accomplish in our lives and through us, is truly amazing!

Today I still have a plan, and that is to know and follow God's plan alone.

Killing the Flesh

Question: Do you drive the speed limit?

My answer to this a year ago would have been, "I usually drive nine miles per hour over the speed limit, just enough so as not to get a ticket. And when I'm following someone going faster, I will often follow their lead to keep out of ticket trouble." I was on a mission to get where I was going, and would consequently be pumped up every time I got behind the wheel.

Now, my answer is, "Yes, I drive the speed limit." I set the cruise control within a mile or two right around the posted speed limit and do my best to stay there. I don't make a legalistic, stressful effort to go exactly the speed limit, even though I could. Then I'd be so proud of myself that I'd have lots of room for boasting and that would pose another problem all its own. My goal is to respect the law and the posted speeds. No other single change in my life has killed more of my flesh or brought me more immediate peace than making the simple change to obey the speed limit laws.

Learning to drive the speed limit started with thoughts while driving, like about not driving so fast and about why I was not driving the speed limit. Like all of us, I rationalized my nine-over position with many forms of justification. I'm sure you've heard most of them and can add a few of your own. But the bottom line is that our reasons are just excuses to justify breaking a law that we've been told to obey. For about a month, I experienced increasing discomfort in my spirit every time I was in the car. I didn't want to acknowledge that my thoughts might be God speaking because then I'd need to listen. And I knew He'd tell me to slow down. So I wrestled inside but never directly asked the Lord what He thought.

About that time I had a haircut scheduled. Looking back, the Lord's timing was evident. He had been preparing me to hear Him whether I asked or not. I arrived at the shop early that morning so I had time to stop by and visit one of my friends who worked there. As I walked in her area, she was excitedly sharing with her customer about how the Lord had just spoken strongly to her about driving too fast. He told her that it was disobedient, sinful, and prideful of her to think she was above the law. If she wanted to be stronger in Him and have all that He had for her, she needed to stop speeding around everywhere and obey that law.

Ding, ding, ding, ding, ding!

Sigh.

Okay, Lord, I get the point.

We continued to talk about some of the reasons we felt it was okay to drive fast, but it all boiled down to one basic reason: we felt like it! Who were we hurting anyway? We wanted to get where we were going and get there *now*. And it was our car so we had a right to drive how we wanted. She shared how much it killed her flesh to drive so slowly, yet the Lord had indeed blessed her with more of Himself and an increasing knowledge of and hunger for Him.

So I changed, but not completely. Not at first. I decided that it was okay to be within the don't-get-a-ticket range of about four miles per hour over the limit, to which my husband responded, "You're still speeding."

"But I'm within the grace allowed by the law."

He grinned and shrugged. And the Holy Spirit nudged again. Okay, well, yes, I was still speeding. I had to repent and submit to God's way (obey the law) and give up my way.

As of today, I've been driving the speed limit for over five years now. It still hurts in some places where the road begs for a higher speed limit, or everyone is speeding around you, or they are following on your bumper because they can't pass you. Trips that previously took four hours now take an extra 20 minutes. My flesh continues to die daily, and at times it goes kicking and screaming.

But the exchange is an incredible amount of peace. I no longer need to constantly scan the roads to see where a police car may be. I am no longer frustrated by other drivers who don't drive like I do. My anxiety level while driving has dropped. And best of all, with each day of death to my flesh, my sense of God's nearness has increased. I hear Him more clearly, I talk to Him more regularly, and our times in the car are just plain sweet.

Question: Will you drive the speed limit?

Waiting … and Waiting … and Waiting …

As I write this chapter, I am in my 50's and still waiting for the Lord to bring me my promised baby. I'm not waiting for an adopted baby, but for a live-birthed baby out of this old womb. I've been holding on to a promise made in 1992, and I even received confirmations along the way that the Lord will indeed do this. Needless to say, it's been a very unusual journey, filled with lots of blessing, disappointment, excitement, discouragement, and pain. Often just when I think I'm okay with not having children, the Lord reveals my heart to me through my circumstances. Over and over again, I have watched other women with the children I didn't have. I have grieved to the point of being in so much pain I couldn't attend a friend's baby shower. Then I reach a place where I'm fine about having no children and I happily move along. Then another new birth close to home, and wham, I'm right back down again.

Finally, the Lord revealed to me the source of my pain: envy! I am the oldest of four children; and, unlike the others, I had been through two marriages and divorces. At a time when I had been single for almost ten years, my three siblings were all married (all first marriages), and two of the three had children. That particular Thanksgiving, I was full of the Lord and His goodness, and finally felt content with everything going on in my life, including my singleness. I had a great church, good friends, a fruitful career, and an awesome relationship with the Lord.

Yes indeed-ee, I was one thankful chick! In fact, I was so thankful that I was bursting at the seams to share at dinner. As is our custom, each person shares something for which they are thankful. I joyfully bubbled over with how much the Lord was doing in my life and how content I was at that moment—husband or not!

Then I discovered that my bubble of joy was amazingly and surprisingly fragile. It burst right then and there with just a few simple words uttered thankfully by my brother-in-law, Tim.

"I'm thankful," he said, "that my wife is going to have a baby next year." As everyone took in what he meant, tears flowed around the table. Wow, the baby of the family was having a baby! I couldn't believe it!

The rest of the dinner was a blur. In fact, the rest of the weekend was a depressing, angry haze. I managed to paste on a smile and shed some tears, but inside I was seething, *How could You do this to me, God? Now everyone in my family is not only married, but they will also all have children. Some God You are!*

My mom, bless her heart, tried to help by acknowledging that it must be hard for me to hear this. That helped a little, but the facts are the facts, and the only One who could have made it better was silent.

As I drove home, I lamented to the Lord. *You just have no* idea *how much this hurts,* (as if He didn't know). He responded immediately and firmly, *It's not hurt, it's envy, and you need to take it to the Cross.*

Talk about the proverbial cold water in the face. My tears instantly dried, and I knew in my heart He spoke exactly the truth that I needed to hear.

Without delay, I repented and chose to bless my sister. Just as immediately as He spoke, the bitterness, hurt, and anger vanished. In their place my heart was filled with love for her and excitement about her news. The whole exchange took less than five minutes.

I'd like to say this was the end of my envy of women with children, but only recently have I truly been able to say, like Paul, that I am content with or without. Yes I have victory now, but remember that it took over fifteen years for me to come to this point. If you are also struggling with an issue such as this, don't be hard on yourself when the victory takes time. Just keep facing God, be willing to call sin what it is, repent, and keep on going forward.

Obey and the Feelings will Follow

I remember Charles Stanley saying in one of his teachings, "Obey and the feelings will follow." I have been blessed to experience this very dramatically, not once, but twice.

The first time, I was "righteously" angry with friends who had really put me out. In 1996, Hurricane Fran ripped through Raleigh on a Friday and left a wide path of destruction in its wake. My friends usually hosted a Sunday evening Bible study, and when we showed up at their house the Sunday after the storm, no one was home. They had been at church that morning and hadn't said anything about cancelling. They could have at least had the common courtesy to call us later when their plans changed. We drove all the way out there, a whole fifteen-minute drive, for nothing.

The following Sunday at church, I overheard that they had no power and had gone to stay with family close by. They'd had no way to get in touch with anyone because it was such short notice. Furthermore, they and their children had been forced to stay with family for nearly a week until their power had been restored.

Even after hearing that, I still felt hurt and angry. A little voice inside said, *Ask her how she's doing.*

What? Me? Ask her? She hasn't apologized for not being there, nor has she come to me, so why should I go to her?

But I knew it was the Lord's voice. So even though I still felt angry, I chose to do as He said. After church, I went to their car, leaned in, and said to her, "How are you doing?" Immediately after the words left my mouth, I felt compassion and love for her and felt for what it must have been like to have to pack up your kids, leave your house, and live out of suitcases for almost a week. I was so stunned I missed her answer, but have remembered the impact of that moment to this day.

Years later, my husband Don and I were on the way home from a long trip. I was driving and Don was sleeping. He woke up as I started to get tired and needed a restroom break. I thought, *Good. As soon as I can stop, he can drive and I can sleep.* I didn't try to talk to him yet because he likes time to wake up quietly.

Then his friend called. They talked and talked and talked, right through a stop at the rest area and continued on after he started to drive. I was tired and cranky and all I wanted to do was get some sleep. I laid the seat back and tried to doze off, but the intermittent talking made sleep impossible. After I had driven such a long way and let him sleep and tried to do what he wanted by giving him time to wake up, my flesh was roaring for some justice. Couldn't he see that I was trying to sleep?

I had two choices: A) I could speak out of my flesh with some sarcastic remark and sour face, or B) I could simply ask nicely if he'd be done soon because I wanted to sleep. By some miracle, I chose B. As soon as the words left my mouth, the irritation left my emotions. The change happened so quickly that it startled me. I was no longer angry and actually felt love for Don. He ended his conversation and I laid the seat back to sleep, still amazed at the instant transformation of my emotions.

What these two events taught me yet again is that when we choose to say or do what is right, God's grace is right there to kill the flesh and energize the spirit. Will there always be an emotional change? No. But the only way there can or will be a change is to choose to live by the spirit and not be guided by our emotions.

The Litter Incident

One morning after church, my husband and I ventured out to a local paved greenway trail for a bike ride. The sun was hot, sky blue, breeze cool, trail in excellent condition, symphony of natural sounds all around, and only a few folks out and about. We were enjoying everything about the ride!

Until I spotted it – an empty Dunkin Donuts cup on the side of the trail.

Can you believe it? I thought, with the appropriately condemning shake of my head, *Some people are just so stup—*

They didn't know they dropped it.

Abruptly, the Lord interrupted me. And as only He can do, He graciously revealed to my heart that I was judging again.

Ouch – seriously Lord? I judged them?

Silence.

OK, so someone was careless and not paying attention, and lost their cup...which, yes, they littered. Intentional or not, didn't I have a valid point about litter not being right? Yes. But did I have the right to label them as Head of the Greenway Trail Littering Brigade?

The same is true for many things people do that hurt us: they didn't know. In fact, often times they have no idea that we are hurt, and their action wasn't about us at all! Instead of trying to see from their viewpoint, we often jump to self-centered, snap judgments. All of a sudden, they are Card Carrying Members of the "Against Us" club, guilty until proven innocent...to our satisfaction.

OK, so I understand I need to forgive this person who unintentionally littered. No problem, they'll probably be upset when they realize it. But wait, I also need to forgive them if they intentionally marred the pristine landscape with their trashy and dirty used cup?

Silence.

And what about people who hurt us, Lord, what about them? I understand forgiving someone who makes a mistake, but what if their primary intent was to hurt us? What if they even meant to destroy us? I need to forgive them too?

By this time, I realized my "conversation" was one way. Then I remembered something Jesus said on the cross (paraphrased): "Father, forgive them. They didn't know what they were doing."

Wait, how could they not know they were killing Him? I mean, after all, isn't death the main intent of a crucifixion? So how could Jesus say, "They didn't know what they were doing?"

Maybe it's because He perfectly knew and understood everything about them. He knew how their motives were influenced by their weaknesses, their fears, and their failures. So He knew that in all of their human-ness, there was no way for them to fully "know" what they were doing.

Likewise, He knows each and every one of us, completely and fully, in a way we can't even begin to comprehend. And knowing us, He forgives us too – even when we "know better" than to throw out that litter.

"For God did not send his Son into the world to condemn the world, but to save the world through him." (John 3:17)

So whether another's sin (or littering) is intentional or not, we are called to forgive. We have no right to rush to snap judgment.

Next time I am tempted to jump to conclusions, I hope I remember the Litter Incident!

The Lord Showed Me My Heart

And it was ugly.

When I arrived at work one day, I spoke to a co-worker who I'll call Joan, on the way in from the parking lot. She hardly paused long enough to listen, then answered over her shoulder as she continued to walk by.

Not to be discouraged, I went to her desk a few minutes later to continue the conversation. I thought maybe she needed to get inside quickly for some reason and that's why she didn't stop to chat. Found out from her continued brief responses that, no, she just didn't want to talk to me.

Crushed and heart-broken, I went back to my desk. I've seen Joan enjoy friendly conversations with others about non-work topics. Since I work somewhat closely with her, I've been trying on and off for a while to "join in" and be friendly too. Her short answers have always bothered me a little, but until today I always managed to shrug them off. But I guess it finally hit me: Joan just doesn't like me personally.

Close to tears, I sat at my desk and talked to the Lord about why it hurt so much this time. I knew I was overreacting because I knew *I* had people I didn't especially like, and I knew it was not realistic to expect everyone to like me.

Yet my heart just hurt so much.

"You know how you are with people you don't particularly like? This is how they feel when you treat them like Joan treated you."

Stunned by His truth, my heart broke even more. Oh my, yes, I've treated others just like this! Oh my, I had no idea! I didn't want to admit it, but I had to face the ugly truth that I was just like Joan. When someone I didn't "like" tried to talk to me and I was not interested, I gave the one-word answers and hurried to get away. And I've always felt bad about it later…but not bad enough to change.

Until now.

Oh Lord, I am so sorry!

In 2 Corinthians 7:10, Paul speaks about repentance: "Godly sorrow brings repentance that leads to salvation and leaves no regret, but worldly sorrow brings death."

Until now, I had experienced worldly sorrow that brought death. I felt sorry for a moment after I mistreated someone, then quickly moved on, leaving a trail of hurt in my wake. But now I experienced godly sorrow that transformed my heart, brought salvation to my sinful brokenness, and left no regret that the Lord had to break my heart to heal it.

In His great mercy, He gave me an immediate opportunity to reveal what He had done and to allow me to experience the joy of my changed heart.

I had a meeting scheduled with a person I had previously shunned. With my new revelation, I waited with excitement for the meeting time so I could welcome him and be friendly to him. My "like" of this person was real and from my heart – my God-changed heart. The difference was nothing short of miraculous.

Once again, I am humbled and amazed at how little it takes from me – just a willing heart and a choice to obey – to receive so much from Him. I cannot change my own heart by "doing" like I can improve my physical fitness through eating right and exercise. To become more spiritually fit, my "doing" is simply to respond in obedience when He initiates – He does the inside changing. I rest in Him, He works in me.

Oh, the glorious life of walking with Jesus!

That day at work the Lord showed me my ugly heart. I'm so glad He did!

Close Enough

Close enough is okay when you're describing an event but miss a few details.

Close enough is okay when you're parallel parking.

Close enough is even okay when you're hanging a picture and you're not quite at the center of the wall.

But close enough is not okay when it comes to obeying God.

Last night I put the finishing touches on my submission for a book contest. As I read my entry for the last time, I paused at the line, "written in short chapters for people who don't like to read." Wow, really? Writing a book for people who don't like to read? They'll think that's crazy. I know it was the Lord who told me to write books for people who don't like to read...but they don't need to know that.

What about, "written in short chapters for people who don't have much time to read?" That made much more sense, and it's a more acceptable reason. And it's close enough to what the Lord told me. Change made, I sent it in.

First thing on my mind when I woke up this morning: changing that sentence. Immediately following that thought, a question: *But so what, Lord? It's such a small change, isn't it close enough? Do they really care, one way or another?*

They may not care, but I do. It's not what I told you to say.

Yes, it's a small thing. And yes, it probably didn't matter to the quality of the overall entry. But since it was directly disobedient to what God told me, I had to correct it. Partial obedience is disobedience. I changed my wording back to the original, and sent in my revised entry.

And God wasn't done with me yet.

I talked to a friend of mine on the way into work this morning. As I pulled into my parking space at 7:55, I let her know I was at work and had to go. She was talking about an incident with her neighbor, and sharing prayer needs. I really wanted to get into work because I had a busy day, but she was still going into the details of her story.

After a few minutes, I finally cut her off with, "I'm sorry, but I've really got to run because I have a meeting at 8 o'clock." So we quickly said good-bye and I went into work.

Only one small problem: I didn't have a meeting at 8 o'clock. Well, I had work to do and had scheduled that time for a particular task. Wasn't that close enough?

No, I lied. Whatever the reason and whatever the motive, a lie is a lie. Even after a fresh lesson on obeying in the small things, I quickly and easily blurted out a lie to make myself sound more acceptable. Again. How quickly I fell.

But God! He's always there with forgiveness, correction, and courage to do the right thing...if only we are willing to reject close enough and obey Him.

I texted my friend, explained that I didn't really have a meeting but just wanted to get into work, and asked for her forgiveness. She understood. She forgave me. Yes, she's a good friend, and I'm thankful for her.

And I'm thankful for my Father who cares enough about me to teach me and correct me in the little things...and that I'm close enough to hear His voice when He does.

Challenge Questions:

1) Who is your most encouraging Bible character? Why are you encouraged by his/her life?

2) What "God stories" do you have? What has God done for you recently? What is your favorite "God story?"

3) What testimony have you read or heard lately from someone else's life that has encouraged you to grow closer to God?

7

FINAL CHALLENGE

I HOPE AND PRAY the Lord has spoken to you as you've read this book, and that you've been encouraged.

As human beings, we are all alike in three fundamental ways. First, we all have breath—we're alive. Next, we all have 24 hours in a day, seven days a week, and 52 weeks in a year—the same amount of time no matter who we are. And finally, we all have free will—the freedom to choose how we will spend that time, and thereby choosing what we will build with our lives and who we will become.

The first choice we must make before we can enjoy a relationship with God or grow in spiritual fitness is to become a Christian. By Christian, I mean a true follower and disciple of Jesus and not just claiming to be a Christian because your family is Christian or you attend church. If you either know you aren't a Christian or you're not sure, read Romans 3:23, Romans 6:23, John 3:1-21, John 14:6, Romans 10:9-10, 1 John

1:5-10, and Ephesians 2:8-10. As Jesus, Paul, and John tell us, salvation requires us to 1) believe that Jesus is who He says He is; 2) confess that you are a sinner and need Jesus; and 3) repent and change who is in charge of your live by turning from your own way and inviting Jesus to be Lord over your life. If you are ready, pray with all your heart for God to forgive your sins, accept what Jesus did on the cross for you, and ask for and receive new life in the Holy Spirit.

Not sure how to pray? Ask God to give you the words; then, in faith, just pray what comes to your mind. Or you can simply pray "Jesus, I want you and need you. Come into my life and take over."

If you've just prayed to become a Christian, welcome to the family! The angels in heaven are rejoicing over your salvation. And God is beaming, arms open wide to welcome you into His embrace. Take some time to thank Him for what He's done for you and enjoy His presence. Then ask the Holy Spirit to guide you to a good local church where you can proclaim what you've done and begin your journey with other believers who can encourage and support you.

If you're not a Christian and not yet ready, keep asking and seeking. God is always by your side, always revealing Himself to you and waiting for you to respond. But again, realize that growing in a spiritual faith and in a relationship with God without ever choosing to become a Christian is just as impossible as growing in physical stature without ever having been born.

My final challenge is to Christians who all have in common the same Holy Spirit living inside of us. That means we are all equally empowered to make right choices, avoid temptation, and spend time knowing God more fully. To grow in spiritual fitness, these are the basic requirements: Allow the Holy Spirit to empower you, and choose to give God all of your life, every moment of every day. I challenge you to take time today to meet with God and prayerfully make your plan. Ask Him to guide you, and let Him set the terms. As He's shown me and is longing to show you, He does a much better job of running our lives than we ever could. Give Him your all, and He'll give you His.

I can promise you, you will not be disappointed!

MEET THE AUTHOR

Mary Graziano Scro is an inspirational and entertaining author and speaker who intuitively weaves analogies and personal testimony with practical biblical teaching. Mary lives with her husband, Don, in Marshall, VA., where they enjoy life with family.

The mission of Mary's ministry, Life is Not a Formula, is to encourage, equip, and exhort believers to pursue a life of obedience (John 8:31) so they can be set free by the truth (John 8:32). God has an awesome life planned for each one of us, if only we are willing to choose His way instead of ours. And it's not just about us – the more we invest in our own unique relationship with Jesus, the more visible He is to a world that desperately needs Him.

This is Mary's first book, and she has many more planned. By openly sharing God stories from her own life, both successes and failures, Mary's desire is to inspire others that if she can be healed, transformed, and set free to enjoy life to the full, they can too!

You can contact Mary at *Mary@LifeisNotaFormula.com*, or visit her website, www.LifeIsNotaFormula.com.

Discover more books and learn about our new approach to publishing at **VoxDeiPublishing.com.**

Made in the USA
Charleston, SC
14 December 2015